Lerner Wildlife Library

Animals of
the POLAR REGIONS

written by Sylvia A. Johnson
illustrated by Alcuin C. Dornisch

Lerner Publications Company
Minneapolis, Minnesota

LIBRARY OF CONGRESS CATALOGING IN PUBLICATION DATA

Johnson, Sylvia A.
    Animals of the polar regions.

    (Lerner Wildlife Library)
    SUMMARY: Discusses the habits of ten animals that live
in the polar regions: the walrus, polar bear, barren-ground caribou, arctic lemming, musk ox, snowy owl, arctic tern, arctic
hare, arctic fox, and emperor penguin. Also includes introduc-
tory material describing these two regions.

    1. Zoology—Polar regions—Juvenile literature. [1. Zoology
—Polar regions. 2. Animals—Habits and behavior. 3. Polar
regions] I. Dornisch, Alcuin C. II. Title.
QL104.J63 1976   599'.09'98   75-27753
ISBN 0-8225-1281-5

Published simultaneously in Canada by
J. M. Dent & Sons (Canada) Ltd., Don Mills, Ontario

Manufactured in the United States of America

International Standard Book Number: 0-8225-1281-5
Library of Congress Catalog Card Number: 75-27753

Second Printing 1977

Contents

Animals of the POLAR REGIONS

The cold and empty regions at the top and bottom of the world are mysterious places far removed from the lives and the imaginations of most people. Although human beings have known for centuries that these areas existed, it was not until the first part of the 20th century that explorers were actually able to penetrate deep into the polar regions and to reach the North and South poles. Since the time of the earliest polar explorations, we have learned a great deal about the north and south polar regions. Scientists have studied the climates and the characteristics of the areas and have marked off the boundaries that separate them from other regions. For many scientists, these boundaries are ones that are measured in terms of light.

Light behaves strangely in the polar regions due to a basic fact about the planet Earth: it is *tilted* on its axis, the imaginary line through the center of the earth around which the planet rotates. As the earth moves through the sky in its yearly orbit around the sun, its tilted position causes first one polar region and then the other to be slanted in the direction of the sun. When the North Pole is tilted toward the sun during summer in the Northern Hemisphere, the very top of the world receives six months of continuous sunlight. At the same time, the South Pole is hidden by six months of darkness. During the other half of the year, the situation is reversed: winter darkness covers the North Pole, and the South Pole has a six-month-long summer day.

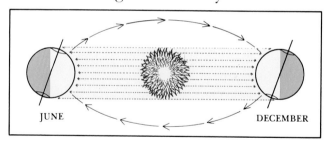

JUNE　　　　　　　　　DECEMBER

It is only at the poles themselves that the periods of light and dark last six months. Moving away from the poles, the periods become gradually shorter until a point is reached where there is only one 24-hour period of continuous sunlight and one 24-hour period of continuous darkness during each year. At these levels around the top and bottom of the world, scientists have drawn imaginary lines, which serve to mark off the boundaries of the two polar regions. The line around the North Pole is called the Arctic Circle, and above it is the north polar region, or simply the Arctic. At the bottom of the world is the Antarctic Circle, and below it, the vast area of the Antarctic—the south polar region.

Located at opposite ends of the earth, the two polar regions are alike in their long days of darkness and light, but they are different in many other ways. The most significant difference lies in the basic physical characteristics of each area. The north polar region is made up of a small ocean—the Arctic Ocean —which is surrounded by several large continents; the south polar region consists of a small continent—Antarctica—which is surrounded by a great deal of water. (The maps on the next page show the territory included within the two polar regions.)

Antarctica, the second smallest of the world's continents, is a mountainous area of land with an average altitude of 6,000 feet (1,800 meters) and an average yearly temperature around zero degrees Fahrenheit (-18 degrees Celsius). Most of this high, cold land is covered by a sheet of ice and snow at least one mile (1.6 kilometers) thick. Only on the very edges of the continent are there any areas that are free

from ice, and it is in these areas that the limited plant life of the Antarctic can be found —large numbers of primitive plants such as mosses and lichens (LI-kuns), and only three species of flowering plants. Because there are so few plants in the Antarctic, there are also very few animals that live on the land and that depend directly on plants for food. In fact, insects are the only animals that can survive in the interior of Antarctica. But there are many kinds of creatures whose homes are in the ocean or whose food comes from this source—fish, whales, seals, and thousands of birds, including the famous Antarctic penguins. Some of these animals spend part of their lives in the ocean and part on the great ice pack of frozen ocean water that surrounds Antarctica, extending outward for many miles.

At the top of the world, the Arctic Ocean is also choked with ice during most of the year. The frigid North Pole, located in the center of the ocean, is always covered with a solid pack of ice. Farther south, however, summer temperatures often rise above freezing, causing the ice pack to melt a little and to break into floating sheets of ice called ice *floes* (FLOWS). Summer brings an even more startling change to the land regions of North America, Europe, and Asia that lie

North Polar Region

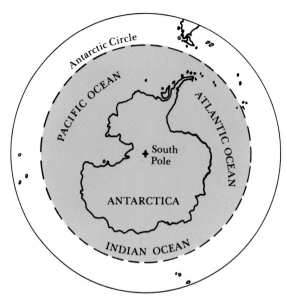

South Polar Region

north of the Arctic Circle. During the summer months of July and August, the winter snows melt, and the flat arctic land is exposed to the warmth of the sun. The top layer of the frozen soil thaws out, and green plants push their way to the surface. In this far northern land, called the *tundra*, the growing season is short, but it provides enough warmth for the development of many kinds of lichens, grasses, flowers, and even bushes and shrubs. (Trees, of course, cannot survive in the severe arctic climate.) The plant life of the tundra in turn supports a large number of animals of all kinds and sizes—small rodents and large grazing animals that feed on the tundra vegetation, and predators like the arctic fox and the polar bear, who eat the flesh of other creatures.

The animals of the Arctic and the Antarctic live in two of the most difficult environments in the world. In the harsh climates of the polar regions, the necessities of animal life— food, shelter, the opportunity to reproduce— are often difficult to obtain. Yet the creatures of the polar regions are somehow able to survive and to thrive despite such difficulties.

Emperor Penguin

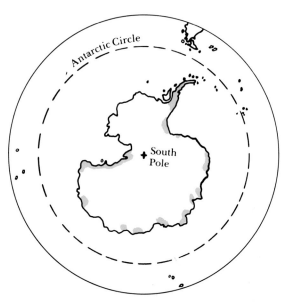

The beautiful emperor penguins (*Aptenodytes fosteri*), largest members of the penguin family, make their home in the cold regions south of the Antarctic Circle. These amazing flightless birds have many unusual habits, but none quite so unusual as the manner in which they produce their young. The emperors' breeding season begins in March, the month that brings the end of the brief antarctic summer. Leaving the waters of the icy sea, the penguins move toward their breeding grounds, located on the coast of Antarctica. When they reach their destination, the male and female penguins seek mates, going through elaborate courtship ceremonies in which the birds serenade each other with melodic songs. Courtship is followed by mating, and each female lays a single egg in April, when the fierce antarctic winter is closing in. Very soon after the egg is laid, the female leaves it in her mate's care and hurries off to feed, after having gone a month without food. During the next 60 days, the male penguin has sole responsibility for the precious egg. Since emperor penguins do not have nests, the male holds the egg balanced on his large webbed feet to keep it off the cold ice. The egg is covered and kept warm by a fold of skin that hangs down from the penguin's stomach. While the temperature drops to 60 degrees below zero and storm winds howl, all the male emperors in the group huddle together for protection and warmth. They do not eat during the long days of their vigil, and by the time that their mates return, the male penguins may have lost up to 40 percent of their body weight. When the females rejoin the males, the eggs are ready to hatch into fluffy gray penguin chicks. Each female feeds her chick with food stored in her body and makes a place for it on her own feet, while her starving mate goes off to a well-deserved meal of fish and shrimp.

Arctic Lemming

One of the most common animals in the Arctic is the arctic lemming (genus *Dicrostonyx*), a little rodent that lives on the tundra both summer and winter. During the summer, lemmings scurry through the matted growth of tundra grass, forming tunnels and runways that extend for miles. During the long arctic winter, the rodents find protection under the tundra's heavy blanket of snow. They spend most of their time in the air space that exists between the layer of snow and the frozen soil underneath. This air space, created by the insulating effect of the snow cover, provides a warm, safe refuge for the little animals. Thus protected, the lemmings live through the winter, until spring arrives, and with it the season of mating and giving birth. Lemmings are champions in matters of reproduction;

each female produces several litters during the spring and summer, each litter containing six or seven baby lemmings. Scientists have discovered that every three or four years, the lemming population of the Arctic is unusually large. There are bumper crops of baby lemmings, and lemming-eating predators such as foxes and owls have an oversupply of food. But the lemmings themselves soon run short of food in their home territory and are forced to move elsewhere in order to find something to eat. The migrating lemmings stream over the land in vast numbers, and nothing stands in their way. When they come to a body of water, they plunge in and swim to the other side. Sometimes, however, the lemmings jump into a river or an arm of the ocean that is too wide for them to cross. Then thousands of the little animals drown, not victims of suicide, as many people think, but simply of a mistake in judgment. After all the uproar of a lemming population explosion is over, the lemming birth rate drops drastically and then begins to climb slowly until it reaches another peak three or four years later. When this happens, the lemmings of the Arctic are in for another season of record births and deaths.

Walrus

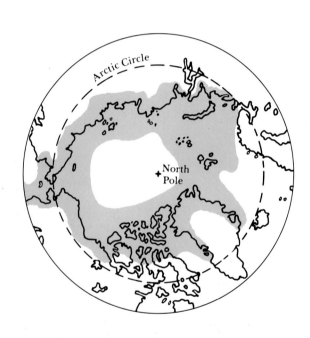

The large and wrinkled walrus (*Odobenus rosmarus*) is one of the many kinds of seals that live in the Arctic. Walruses and other seals belong to the group of mammals known as *pinnipeds*—fin-footed creatures. Like all its relatives, the walrus has two sets of fins or flippers, which are used for swimming. The walrus's hind flippers can be turned forward so that the huge animal can also use them like feet for walking on land. Actually, walruses waddle more than they walk, and they don't often do their waddling on dry land. When they are not in the water, they spend most of their time on the ice floes that float in the Arctic Ocean. Here they rest and sleep in snowstorms or in sunshine, lying close together in cozy groups. Walruses usually live in herds and are very seldom alone, except when they are searching for food. When a walrus wants something to eat, it dives off the ice floe and swims to the ocean bottom. Standing on its head in the water, the walrus digs for the clams that are its favorite food, using its long tusks to pry the clam shells off of the ocean floor. Because the tusks are so important in the walrus's food gathering, young walruses are not able to search for food until their tusks have developed. For the first two years of its life, a walrus pup drinks only its mother's rich milk. Just about the time that one youngster is old enough to dig for its own food, the walrus mother gives birth to a new pup, a 100-pound baby with a bristly moustache and wrinkled skin just like its parents.

Musk Ox

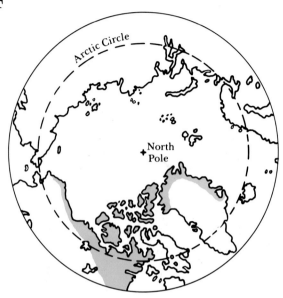

Protection against the cold is important for all the animals that live in the Arctic, and no polar inhabitant is quite so well protected as the sturdy musk ox (*Ovibos moschatus*). This large grazing animal has a magnificent coat of long, heavy hair that provides shelter and warmth in the face of fierce polar winds. Under this outer coat of hair is a wooly undercoat that gives extra warmth. The musk ox needs all the warmth that its thick hair can provide, for during the long arctic winter the animal stays in its cold northern pastures instead of moving south as do some other arctic grazers like the caribou. When snow blankets the empty tundra, the musk ox simply moves to high ground, where the blowing wind uncovers the grass and moss

on which the animal feeds. At the end of the long, dark winter, when temperatures are still well below zero, the female musk ox gives birth to her calf, a wooly-coated little creature weighing less than 20 pounds (nine kilograms). For the first four months of its life, the calf huddles under its mother's long hair and drinks her warm milk, which provides its only nourishment. During this period, the lives of the young musk oxen are threatened not only by the harsh climate but also by attacks from predators such as the powerful arctic wolf. When a herd of musk oxen is attacked by a wolf, the older animals quickly form a protective circle with the calves in the center. Facing outward, their large heads and sharp curved horns turned toward the wolf, the musk oxen stand ready to defend themselves and their young against any threat. Only a very determined and hungry predator risks its life against such effective resistance. But human hunters sometimes use guns to kill the adult animals in the circle and capture the musk ox calves for display in zoos. The ancient defense system of the musk ox is useless against the weapons of human animals.

Barren-ground Caribou

The horned and hooved mammal known as the caribou (CARE-uh-boo) lives in the cold northern territory all around the North Pole. In the Old World, members of the caribou family have been tamed by humans and renamed *reindeer*. The caribou of the New World still run wild in the Arctic regions of North America. One species, the barren-ground caribou (*Rangifer tarandus*), has become famous for the long migrations that it makes twice a year. The barren-ground caribou spends the summer on the broad expanses of the tundra, where the animals feed on the leaves of green plants coaxed into bloom by the brief warmth of the summer sun. As the days become shorter and the weather grows colder, the caribou begin to

gather in large herds and to migrate toward the forest regions that border the tundra to the south. This dense northern forest, known as the taiga (TIE-gah), will provide a refuge for the animals during the cold winter months. Before the caribou go deep into the forest, they first seek mates, the males fighting over the females with their heavy, spreading antlers. After mating has taken place, the herd of caribou enters the forest and begins the serious business of finding food through the cold, snow-filled winter months. Using their enormous feet, the animals scrape the snow away to feed on the lichens that grow on the forest floor. By April, the ground is still covered with snow, but the severest part of the winter is over, and the caribou are on the move once again. The females leave first, traveling north to the calving grounds that they have used in seasons past. There they give birth to their young, one or two calves to each mother. By the time that the caribou calves are steady on their feet and ready for travel, the male caribou have rejoined the herd. Then the animals move north in vast numbers to their summer pastures on the tundra.

Arctic Fox

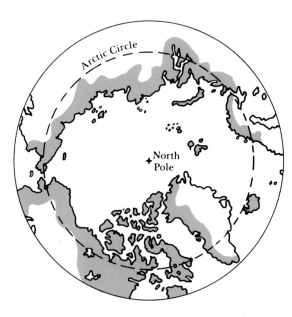

Foxes make their homes in many kinds of environments—in dense woodlands, in grassy fields, in arid deserts. The snowy regions of the Far North are also inhabited by a member of the fox family, the beautiful arctic fox (*Alopex lagopus*). During the summer, the arctic fox wears a tawny-colored coat similar to those of its relatives in warmer parts of the world. But when winter comes, its color changes to a pure white that matches the snowy winter landscape and makes the little fox hard to see. The arctic fox's outer fur is long and fluffy, serving as an air-filled insulator against the bitter cold. Next to its skin is a fuzzy undercoat that provides additional warmth. The rest of the arctic fox's body is also designed for cold-weather comfort: small, round ears that allow little body heat to escape; fur-covered feet that serve as ready-made snowshoes; and a fluffy tail that can be used as a blanket on cold winter nights. The arctic fox is well prepared for winter cold, but food can sometimes be a problem during the long winter months. Lemmings are the main dish on the fox's menu, and when these little rodents are plentiful, the arctic fox eats well. During years of lemming population explosions, the foxes have more than enough food, and the well-fed adults often produce record numbers of baby foxes the following year. But when lemmings are scarce, the arctic fox must search hard for its food. During especially harsh winters, the foxes often trail after larger predators such as polar bears and wolves, hoping to share in the leftovers of their meals. Survival does not come easy in the arctic fox's difficult environment.

Arctic Tern

(*Sterna paradisaea*). This amazing bird is the only creature that is native to both the north and the south polar regions. It spends a small part of the year in each area and the rest of its time flying over the long distance in between. When the arctic summer begins its slow awakening in June, the arctic tern arrives at its nesting grounds near the North Pole. Like many other species of birds, it comes to the Arctic to mate and lay its eggs, taking advantage of the long days of summer sunlight and the abundance of insects. After the young terns hatch from their eggs, they develop very quickly, and by August or September, when winter is approaching, they are ready to start on a long journey. Leaving the Arctic, the terns fly south to the bottom of the world. Their journey takes seven months, and by the time they reach the South Pole, the antarctic summer has begun. The birds spend a short time in the continuous sunshine of another polar summer and then take off again to return to the Far North. After flying over 8,000 miles, they reach the Arctic nesting grounds just in time to mate and lay eggs, and to begin the incredible cycle once again.

The polar regions of the earth are separated by thousands of miles, and though they are alike in the coldness of their climates, they are very different in other ways. Yet despite the distance and the differences that set them apart, the Arctic and the Antarctic are bound together by a unique animal, the arctic tern

Arctic Hare

The arctic hare (*Lepus arcticus*) is another animal of the Far North that changes the color of its coat twice a year. During the summer, most arctic hares wear coats of brownish fur to match the quiet colors of the barren tundra. But when winter comes, and with it the heavy snows, their fur changes to pure white. (A few arctic hares that live in areas always covered with snow wear white coats all year round.) The arctic hares' system of color camouflage provides the animals with some protection against the wolves and other hungry predators that hunt them for food. Of course, arctic hares themselves are vegetarians, as are all other hares and rabbits.

They feed on the grasses and plants of the tundra both summer and winter. Finding food during the summer months is easy, but winter feeding is more of a challenge. In order to eat and to survive, the hares must dig through the hard crust of snow that covers the tundra. The animals' large feet and broad front teeth make good digging tools, and their sensitive noses help them to locate nourishing twigs and grasses buried under the snow. During most of the year, arctic hares live in groups, feeding together and wandering over the tundra. When the spring mating season arrives, however, the hares are not so friendly. The males engage in combat with each other, standing on their hind legs and hitting their opponents with their powerful front feet. After the contests are over and mating has taken place, the female hares leave the herd and go off on their own. About a month later, the baby hares are born, with wide-open eyes and full coats of fur. The young hares grow very quickly, and soon they are ready to join their parents in searching for food and avoiding the predators that continually threaten their lives.

Polar Bear

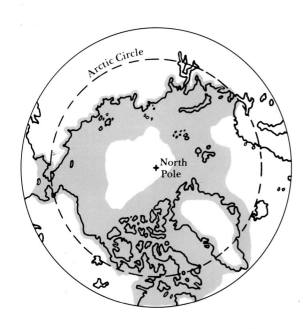

All bears are skilled at hunting, but the polar bear (*Tharlarctos maritimus*) is the outstanding hunter of the bear family. This inhabitant of the frozen Arctic depends on its hunting skills, for its primary source of food is the flesh of the other animals that share its environment. Polar bears make their homes on the pack ice that floats in the icy waters of the Arctic Ocean. During the warmer months of the arctic year, the bears prey on the seals that live in the open waters surrounding the floating ice. The fierce hunters prowl endlessly over the ice floes, their keen eyes searching for the dark form of a seal that has climbed up out of the water to rest or to bask in the sun. When a polar bear spots a seal, it begins to stalk its prey. Flattening out on the ice, the bear moves soundlessly toward the seal, pulling itself forward with its fur-covered front feet. The predator's yellowish-white coat blends in perfectly with its surroundings, and the bear conceals itself further by hiding behind every available outcropping of ice. During the dark arctic winter, when there are fewer areas of open water and seals spend most of the time under the ice, the polar bear must use a different means of catching its prey. Then a hunting bear waits patiently near a hole in the ice where seals come up to snatch a breath of air. When a seal puts in an appearance, the polar bear tries to seize the animal before it can disappear beneath the ice. Sometimes its efforts are unsuccessful, and the seal will plunge back into the safety of the water. Often enough, however, the bear will catch its victim and obtain the energy-giving meal of meat and fat so essential to its survival in the cold Arctic.

Snowy Owl

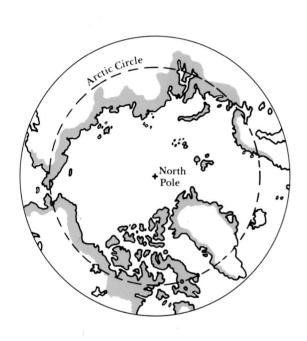

Many birds come to the Arctic to breed and nest, but only a few species spend the whole year in the Far North. Among these few hardy birds is the snowy owl (*Nyctea scandiaca*). This large and beautiful member of the owl family lives on the tundra the year round, during winter storms and summer thaws. A hunter like all owls, the snowy owl feeds on the lemmings and other small rodents that share its homeland. The feathered predator hunts only at night, using its keen eyesight and hearing to locate prey scurrying through the tundra grasses or over the blanket of winter snow. The snowy owl, like all its relatives, is an efficient hunter and consumer, able to make good use of the resources available in its environment. There are times, however, when the snowy owl's resources fail. During winters when the lemming population is low, the owls are often forced to leave their home territory and to seek food in the taiga or even further south. But no matter how far away the owls must go, by spring they will be back on the tundra and ready for the season of mating and egg-laying. The female snowy owl lays her eggs on the ground in a slight hollow lined with moss. During the time that she sits on the eggs to keep them warm, her mate will do the hunting for two, bringing food to his motion-less partner. In about a month, the eggs break open and the baby owls come tumbling out into the cold arctic world. The owlets are covered with fluffy white down that soon changes to a soft grey and then to the elegant white and brown feathers of the adult owls.

Scale of Animal Sizes

Emperor Penguin
Aptenodytes fosteri

Arctic Lemming
Genus *Dicrostonyx*

Walrus
Odobenus rosmarus

Musk Ox
Ovibos moschatus

Barren-ground Caribou
Rangifer tarandus

Arctic Fox
Alopex lagopus

Arctic Tern
Sterna paradisaea

Arctic Hare
Lepus arcticus

Polar Bear
Thalarctos maritimus

Snowy Owl
Nyctea scandiaca

 = *1 Foot*    = *1 Meter*   *Animals of the Polar Regions*

599
JOH
C. 1
Johnson, Sylvia
A.

Animals of the
polar regions

DATE			